Original title:
Crafting Creativity

Copyright © 2024 Swan Charm Publishing
All rights reserved.

Editor: Jessica Elisabeth Luik
Author: Liina Liblikas
ISBN HARDBACK: 978-9916-86-262-9
ISBN PAPERBACK: 978-9916-86-263-6

Tales from the Artisan's Hearth

In the glow of amber light,
Crafts are born in silent night.
Fingers dance with gentle grace,
Shaping dreams in time's embrace.

Wood and metal, clay and thread,
Stories in each line are read.
Whispers of an age gone by,
Echo softly, time slips by.

Fire's warmth, a mystic guide,
Where creation does reside.
Hearts and hands in concert, play,
Molding visions into clay.

By the hearth, the artisan stands,
With age-old tools in weathered hands.
From simple starts to grand design,
Legacy in every line.

In every flaw, perfection's seed,
Echoes of a soul set free.
Tales from the hearth take their flight,
Crafted in the tranquil night.

Compositions of Light

In brilliant hues, morning breaks,
Awakening the world's facade.
Ripples of dawn on the lakes,
Crafting dreams both near and broad.

Crystal shards on dew-kissed grass,
Reflecting hopes anew.
Whispers of the day amass,
Guiding hearts with steady view.

Golden rays in endless sprawl,
Painting skies with grace.
With every shadow, answers call,
In ethereal light's embrace.

Echoes of Imagination

In the silent chambers of the mind,
Visions dance and play.
Worlds unseen begin to find,
Their paths to light of day.

Waves of wonder crash and roll,
On shores of thought's domain.
From the depths, new stories pull,
In endless, boundless chain.

Starry nights reveal their tales,
Of realms both wild and free.
Cascades of dreams leave trails,
For every soul to see.

Reflections from the Forge

In the heart of molten fire,
Shapes of iron are born.
Crafted by a firm desire,
To weather every storm.

Hammers ring in steady beat,
An anthem to creation.
Sparks that jump from furnace heat,
Speak of transformation.

Steel and courage intertwine,
Fate is met with trust.
Each formed piece, a design,
From ember's bloom to ash and dust.

Divine Inspirations

From the heavens, whispers flow,
To those who seek and wait.
Sacred streams of wisdom show,
In moments small and great.

Elusive truths in golden light,
Guide the hands of fate.
Blessings in the silent night,
Their echoes resonate.

Through the veil, the spirits call,
To hearts open and true.
In divine grace, we find our all,
In every dawn's debut.

Mind's Mosaic

Upon the canvas of the mind,
A tapestry of thoughts we find.
Fragments of past and dreams unspun,
A mosaic dances in the sun.

Colors weave and memories blend,
Imagination knows no end.
In this space of vast creation,
Lies the heart of inspiration.

From chaos comes a vivid hue,
Each piece unique, yet tied to you.
In every shard, a story told,
A mosaic bright, a sight to hold.

The Birth of Notions

In the quiet of the eve,
Thoughts like whispers interweave.
Seeds of wonder softly sown,
In the fertile, unseen zone.

From the silence, ideas spring,
Like the flutter of a wing.
Glimmers of potential rise,
Lighting up the darkest skies.

Every notion, new and pure,
A creation to endure.
In the mind's eye, they ignite,
Endless dawns of sheer delight.

Whispers of Brilliance

Gentle voices in the night,
Hint of brilliance, sharp and bright.
Softly spoken, wisdom flows,
In the hushed, celestial prose.

Inspiration subtly speaks,
Guiding those who truth seeks.
In the quiet, find the spark,
Lighting beacons in the dark.

Listen closely to the air,
Brilliance whispers everywhere.
In each murmur find the key,
To unlock infinity.

Crafting Luminary Paths

With each step, a trail is blazed,
Through the fog, no longer dazed.
Light from heart and mind combined,
Crafts a path that's well-defined.

In the journey, courage finds,
Ways to open wary minds.
Brilliant paths of radiant glow,
From within, the light will flow.

Every stride with purpose pure,
Makes the unknown future sure.
In each path a dream, a start,
Crafted from a glowing heart.

The Designer's Dreamscape

In a world-built pixel by pixel,
Where fantasy and reality entwine,
Colors splash in vibrant mosaic,
As visions birth from a gridded line.

Blueprints speak in silent whispers,
Sketches breathe with promised life,
Every layer a realm unfolding,
Untangling chaos, fending off strife.

Symmetry dances, balanced, poised,
Textures weave stories untold,
Patterns pulse with coded rhythms,
As creativity erases the old.

Vistas bloom in endless circuits,
Circuitous pathways perpetually bloom,
Dreams transmute into virtual realms,
Awakening in digital wombs.

Crafting Illusions

Mirror's edge, where truths dissolve,
Reality's veil spins thin,
Crafted worlds of shifting sands,
Illusions where dreams begin.

Through the looking glass we step,
Unknown roads bend and weave,
Lost in mazes of our making,
Every step a web to deceive.

Glimmering vistas taunt our eyes,
Fantasies in fragile frames,
Every shadow mocks sincerity,
Deceit resides, wearing false names.

Enigmas bloom in twilight hours,
Crafted myths slowly unfurl,
Summoned forth by the mind's caress,
As illusions become our world.

The Poet's Canvas

Ink flows like rivers on paper,
Words craft landscapes of the soul,
Every verse a brushstroke deep,
Painting lives where hearts console.

Sonnets whisper love's embrace,
Ballads echo tales of yore,
On the canvas of the poet's mind,
Emotions flood, forevermore.

Nature's hues in metaphors,
Stars speak in similes sweet,
The sun rises in rhythmic stanzas,
Moonlight glimmers in a heartbeat.

Uncharted realms in lyric's gaze,
Ephemeral beauty takes its place,
Every poem a world completed,
Touched by time's tender grace.

The Composer's Creation

Notes cascade in symphonic waves,
Harmonies weave in the air,
A universe birthed from silence,
Crafted with meticulous care.

Strings sing with passion's fire,
Keys dance in spirited flight,
Percussion beats the heart's old drum,
Resonating pure delight.

Melodies weave enchanting spells,
Rhythms pulse with lifeblood's flow,
Themes emerge like dawn's first light,
In the composer's fertile crescendo.

Echoes linger on unseen drafts,
Symphonies etch timeless lore,
Every creation a gateway found,
Unlocking existence through sound's door.

The Composer's Brushstrokes

In shadows, melodies conspire,
Under moon's gentle embrace.
Night writes its silent choir,
Stars in an infinite race.

Colors of the unseen,
Paint notes on astral lines.
Through every silver sheen,
A symphony combines.

With gentle nudges,
Dreams set aflame.
Creation grudges,
Yet seeks no name.

Harmony in chaos,
Every sound a plea.
Eternal fresco gloss,
On time's vast sea.

The Artisan's Canvas

The artisan's heart wends,
Brush carving stories told,
Through hues the soul sends,
A tapestry unfolds.

Ever shifting blend,
Of canvas into light,
Where passions transcend,
Eclipsing day and night.

Each stroke, a lifetime,
In fields of quiet ease,
Color in perfect rhyme,
Setting the spirit free.

Emotions start to dance,
In palettes wide and grand,
A timeless, broad expanse,
Crafted by steady hand.

Symphony of Whispers

In the forest's verdant shade,
Whispers softly swell.
Leaves in breezes played,
Nature's quiet spell.

Streams sing lullabies,
In the moon's fair sheen.
Owls, with knowing eyes,
Survey a world serene.

Every creature's part,
In symphony so grand.
Heartbeats start to chart,
The rhythm of the land.

Silent whispers weave,
In twilight's tender glow.
Echoes softly grieve,
With secrets we may know.

Innovator's Quilt

Threads of idea bound,
In tapestry of gold.
New visions to be found,
Stories yet untold.

Colors vibrant, bright,
In patterns ever shifting.
Weaving day and night,
Dreams aloft, uplifting.

Hands craft future's thread,
In patience and finesse.
Merging paths once tread,
Into seamless dress.

Time and genius blend,
In textile rich and vast.
Innovations send,
Reflections of the past.

The Sculptor's Secret

With chisel sharp, he shapes the stone,
In each soft curve, a world unknown.
His hands reveal what mind conceives,
In marble white, his soul believes.

Whispered secrets hard as rock,
From silent forms, they will unlock.
In each grain, a story told,
Of mysteries in sculptor's hold.

Stone by stone, a life unravels,
Unseen joy and hidden travels.
Echoes from a whisper bare,
He's an artist without compare.

Symphony of Thought

In silent waves, the mind does play,
A symphony of thought, array.
Notes of wisdom, chords of muse,
Melodies in deep hues.

Through the halls of endless reason,
Changing minds like changing seasons.
A song that's born from whispered dreams,
In flowing streams and silvered seams.

Harmony of silent wonder,
Cracking walls that pull us under.
Thoughts do dance, in quiet grace,
In this sacred mental place.

The Writer's Forge

In the writer's forge, a tale is spun,
Fires burn till work is done.
Words as metal, thoughts as flame,
Epics forged in twilight's name.

Hammer blows of ink on page,
Crafting worlds in fervent rage.
Metaphors as sturdy beams,
Supporting realms of dreams.

Quill is sword, and page is shield,
In battles fought, truth's field.
Scripted lines a legacy,
A story cast eternally.

Mosaic of Dreams

In crafted tiles, dreams do gleam,
Colors vast as hopeful scheme.
Each one holds a piece of soul,
Mosaic bright, ambitions' scroll.

Fragmented hopes in perfect blend,
A tapestry with no end.
In each shard, a vision's glow,
Life's grand picture shaped just so.

Dreams in glass, so delicate yet strong,
A place where broken parts belong.
Together they make beauty's theme,
A radiant mosaic of dreams.

Imagination's Alchemy

In chambers of the mind, pure dreams ignite,
Transforming shadows into beams of light.
A flicker turns to gold, the dull to gleam,
In alchemy of hope, we craft our dream.

An ember grows in twilight's whispered song,
A melody where all our hearts belong.
With strokes of thought, we blend the night and day,
In imagination's realm, we find our way.

From ashes rise the visions that we mold,
In cauldrons of the soul, rich tales unfold.
With every spark, new wonders brought to life,
In alchemist's embrace, we conquer strife.

Brushing the Canvas of Dreams

A whisper of blue on morning's first breath,
A stroke of green in the forest's depth.
We paint our worlds in hues both brave and bright,
In the vast canvas where dreams take flight.

With tender strokes, we sketch the unseen,
In every line, our hopes and fears convene.
The brush dips gently in a pool of stars,
Tracing the map to distant lands afar.

In colors bold, our secret wishes blend,
Old wounds and joys on pigments we depend.
Each brush's touch imbues the heart's own tale,
On canvas wide, every fragment prevails.

Invention's Gentle Pulse

In quiet hum of gears, new worlds arise,
From thoughts that spark beneath the star-filled skies.
The gentle pulse of what could be, unfolds,
In webs of light, the future fate foretold.

Invention's whisper speaks in silent dawn,
To minds that dream, new vistas ever drawn.
Each cog and wheel, a promise to aspire,
A dance of steel that kindles the inner fire.

Progress sings in symphonies of code,
In circuits where imagination flowed.
Inventing paths where none had boldly tread,
With every step, to wonders we are led.

Stitching Stories in Air

With every breath, we weave the threads of lore,
In spoken tales, our spirits learn to soar.
Each word a stitch in memory's bright quilt,
In tapestry of time, our lives are built.

Through whispered winds, our stories intertwine,
In shared embrace, our histories align.
In air's soft weave, the past and present meet,
A dance of echoes, life's rhythm incomplete.

We cast our voices to the sky's embrace,
In tales of joy, in sorrow's gentle trace.
In every breeze, the threads of life repair,
Unraveled knots, we mend with tender care.

Brushstrokes of Innovation

Colors blend with thought divine,
Canvas stretched on endless time.
Ideas sparked in hues combine,
Forms emerge, a brilliant climb.

Brush in hand, the mind does race,
Patterns swirl, with vibrant grace.
Each stroke speaks, a silent trace,
Imagination's boundless space.

Vision flows, no chains confine,
Artistry in perfect line.
Brushstrokes dance, in rhythmic sign,
Innovation's pure design.

The Architect of Dreams

Blueprints drawn with finest hand,
Visions rise from desert sand.
Structures bold, with dreams so grand,
Skylines born at mind's command.

Frameworks tower, steel and glass,
Dreams take shape as shadows pass.
Every curve, a thought to amass,
Boundaries pushed, none surpass.

In each line, ambition's gleam,
Architects of grand esteem.
Building worlds from every dream,
Reality flows like a stream.

Glimpses of Brilliance

Moments flicker in the night,
Ideas glowing, burning bright.
Glimpses rare, like stars in sight,
Whispers of a mind's delight.

In the silence, brilliance grows,
Quiet thoughts, in whispers, flow.
Sparks ignite, and quickly show,
Flashes where pure genius glows.

Caught within a fleeting glace,
Inspiration leads the dance.
Moments hold a universe,
Glimpses pure, the mind's advance.

Voices Under the Pen

Ink pours forth, like steady rain,
Words take shape, in endless strain.
Silent voices, thoughts unchain,
Pages tell of joy and pain.

Stories crafted, worlds unfurl,
In each line, emotions swirl.
Voices pen, like pearls in pearl,
Every sentence, hearts twirl.

From the pen, realities spin,
Tales of love, loss, and no sin.
Writing worlds, where dreams begin,
Voices speak, the mind within.

A Dance of Epiphanies

In the quiet dawn, thoughts do awaken,
A tapestry of dreams, softly shaken.
Insight pirouettes, with delicate grace,
Revealing mysteries, in time's embrace.

Moments collide, with whispers profound,
In a symphony, where truths resound.
Ideas swirl, like leaves on the gale,
Each one a spark, igniting the trail.

Shadows recede, with morning's first light,
Glimmers of wisdom, piercing the night.
In the stillness, enlightenment dances,
Unveiling answers, through curious glances.

Whittling Whimsy

With knife in hand, and wood so tender,
Crafting dreams, with a heart so slender.
Each twist and turn, a story unfolds,
In whimsical whispers, new magic molds.

Grain by grain, the shape takes form,
In nature's beauty, a soul is born.
Soft curves emerge, from roughest bark,
In each creation, leaves a mark.

Simple moments, in creative trance,
Lives reimagined, with each glance.
In the artistry of nimble hands,
Whittling whimsy, across shifting sands.

The Alchemy of Ideas

In the cauldron of a curious mind,
Ideas like potions, in thoughts combined.
Alchemy of concepts, blend and fuse,
Creating wonders, in vibrant hues.

From sparks of doubt, to bursts of muse,
Transforming questions, to truths we choose.
Mystic processes, unseen and vast,
Shape our visions, from shadows cast.

Philosophies meld, in the mind's embrace,
Turning leaden fears, to golden grace.
In the alchemy, of endlessly turning wheels,
Ideas become, the magic one feels.

Verses in the Making

Words on paper, dreams unfurl,
Ephemeral thoughts, in ink they twirl.
Lines of meanings, layered and deep,
In verses crafted, memories seep.

Through quiet musings, emotions blend,
Each stanza, a fragment, we intend.
Captured moments, in rhythmic flow,
In silent whispers, our hearts bestow.

Pages filled with, a poet's refrain,
Life's fleeting shadows, joy and pain.
In the making, of verses sublime,
We etch our stories, beyond the time.

Ember of Innovation

In the forge where dreams ignite,
A spark becomes a guiding light.
Boundaries shatter in its blaze,
New paths carved in vibrant haze.

Imagination fuels the flame,
Each thought a wild, untamed frame.
Where vision crafts the future's air,
Possibilities dancing, rare.

Courage kindles every start,
Ideas blaze within the heart.
With each ember, light unfurls,
Innovations change the world.

In this fire, all doubts dissolve,
Challenges met with resolve.
A world transformed by bold creation,
An endless ember's dedication.

From ashes born, brilliance soars,
Endless cycles, open doors.
Ember of innovation's grace,
Illuminates the human race.

Flights of Fancy

Upon the winds of whimsy glide,
The fancies that in hearts reside.
In clouds of dreams, they find their flight,
A tapestry of thoughts alight.

Feathers brush the evening sky,
As visions whisper, drifting by.
Where reality blurs, fantasy reigns,
A world unbound by earthly chains.

In twilight's hue, imaginations bloom,
Their gentle touch dispels the gloom.
With laughter in the realms of mind,
Boundless joy and peace aligned.

Each winged dream, a beacon bright,
Guiding through the moonlit night.
In flights of fancy, souls set free,
On boundless winds of reverie.

Awake within these wondrous airs,
Transcending time, dissolving cares.
Flights of fancy, pure and grand,
In endless realms of dreamland.

The Weaver's Revelation

Strands of life entwine with care,
In loom of fate, beyond compare.
Threads of hope and colors bright,
Woven in the silent night.

Beneath the stars, the weaver's hand,
Crafts a tale across the land.
Patterns rich and stories grand,
Each knot tied by fate's command.

In every weave, a secret shows,
The truth the weaver finely knows.
In tapestry, both joy and pain,
Revealed through every strand's refrain.

Hands that guide with gentle might,
Bringing shadow into light.
A revelation pure and clear,
Woven whispers we all hear.

From warp and weft, a world unfurls,
The weaver's touch, the fate it twirls.
A revelation grand and true,
Life's intricate, eternal view.

Origin of Masterpieces

In silence born, the spark begins,
An artist's muse, where dreams have been.
Upon the canvas, whispers speak,
From heart to hand, their journey seek.

Colors blend in mystic dance,
Each stroke a soul's deep trance.
From chaos, beauty finds its form,
In every hue, a life reborn.

In marble veins, a sculpture wakes,
Lines and curves that heartbeats make.
Chisels carve with tender grace,
Revealing art's eternal face.

Music's notes like rivers flow,
Melodies where passions grow.
Through the strings, emotions rise,
Composing symphonies of skies.

From inspiration's fleeting trace,
Masterpieces find their place.
In origin, a spark ignites,
Creation's endless, wondrous flights.

A Tapestry of Words

Threads of thought in colors bright,
Weaving tales in morning light.
Pages turned, a journey starts,
Bound by words, and open hearts.

Whispers soft, in twilight hues,
Stories old and visions new.
Every line a woven strand,
Crafted by a careful hand.

Mysteries held in folded creases,
Epic tales in tiny pieces.
Let the loom of language spin,
Till the tapestry begins.

Songs of sorrow, notes of bliss,
Every word a fleeting kiss.
In this fabric, every seam,
Fulfills the dreamer's vivid dream.

Sculpting Dreams

From marble blocks and clay's embrace,
We carve out dreams with gentle grace.
A chisel's touch, a vision clear,
A waking world, where dreams appear.

In shadows cast, profound and deep,
Silent forms begin to speak.
Through every curve, and every line,
Emerges art that stands through time.

With molten gold and silver's sheen,
We craft the shapes that others dream.
Evoke the spirit, bold and true,
In statues fixed, yet ever new.

Awake the soul in hardened stone,
In silent monuments alone.
The sculptor's dream, a living art,
In marble veins, a beating heart.

The Weaver's Muse

On looms of thought, we weave our tales,
Through whispered winds and whispered gales.
A fabric rich with dreams enshrined,
By muse's hand, the threads aligned.

Golden threads and silver beams,
Intertwined with hopes and dreams.
Patterned faith and woven lore,
Tell the stories her heart bore.

Colors deep and textures vast,
A weaver's spell of futures past.
In her tapestry of time,
Every stitch a subtle rhyme.

Through the weft and through the warp,
Echo voices clear and sharp.
In the tapestry she weaves,
Live the dreams her soul believes.

Ink and Inspiration

Dark ink flows on paper white,
Igniting thoughts as words take flight.
A poet's pen, a painter's brush,
Turns silent void to vibrant hush.

Dreams are built on parchment here,
Crafted through both hope and fear.
Every scribble, every line,
A masterpiece, where thoughts entwine.

A symphony in silent script,
A world where inner visions lived.
In every stroke, in every form,
Lives a muse in shadowed norm.

From chaos comes a crafted rhyme,
Born of moments, lost in time.
Ink and paper, bound and free,
Inspire hearts through mystery.

Forests of Inspiration

Beneath the emerald canopy,
whispers of leaves in song,
where shadows dance in reverie,
the heart finds where it belongs.

Roots of wisdom crisscross the ground,
secrets from ages past,
every tree, a story unbound,
branches reaching vast.

Birds compose their melodies,
notes on the air, so pure,
each sound a living poiesis,
through twilight's gentle lure.

Streams mirror the poet's dream,
reflecting visions bright,
in the forests, thoughts freely teem,
and day melds into night.

A haven for both heart and mind,
here inspirations swell,
within this grove, a seeker finds,
the words within to tell.

Carving Words from Silence

In the hush of dawn's embrace,
words are gently born,
from silence, they softly trace,
thoughts in creative form.

Night's quiet offers ink and quill,
a canvas vast and wide,
echoes of a world so still,
where whispers softly glide.

Each pause a muse for deeper thought,
a space for minds to weave,
what noise and clamour have forgot,
these recesses believe.

Verses shaped by moments calm,
like sculptures in the night,
carved within this silent psalm,
illuminated by moonlight.

In silence, we craft and build,
with breath and thought combined,
the spaces where our dreams are filled,
and language is defined.

Blooming Ideas

In gardens where ideas bloom,
petals of thought unfurl,
seeds of wonder find their room,
within an endless swirl.

Colors burst in vibrant hues,
concepts fluttering free,
like butterflies amidst the blues,
possibilities we see.

With every dawn, new blooms arise,
from fertile grounds of mind,
creations under open skies,
a treasure trove to find.

Sunlight bathes the growing dreams,
nurtured by the hope within,
each flower in the meadow gleams,
a testament to where we've been.

In this garden, ideas grow,
no limits, bounds, or fears,
a blooming field where rivers flow,
where inspiration steers.

Chasing the Spark

Through shadows and the light,
a spark ignites the soul,
moves like a whisper in the night,
a fire to keep us whole.

Ideas flicker, wane, and gleam,
a chasing dance of flame,
pursue with hope, the visionary dream,
creativity untamed.

Under stars, the spark takes flight,
in the boundless realms of mind,
darkness gives way to brilliant light,
to insights intertwined.

Across the canvas of the night,
bursting from the core,
a journey quest for endless sight,
illumination to explore.

Chasing the spark, through ebb and flow,
we ride the waves of thought,
in every glimmer, a world to know,
to find the truths we've sought.

Harmonies of Creation

In the whisper of dawn's first light,
Where shadows dance and fade,
A symphony of stars takes flight,
In melodies night has made.

Nature hums a timeless tune,
Mountains echo back the call,
River's rush by serene commune,
To oceans vast and tall.

Breezes carry lullabies,
Through forest, field, and fen,
Uniting earth and endless skies,
In songs known to all men.

Each creature joins the grand refrain,
From bird to beast, the song unfolds,
A harmony that knows no strain,
In mysteries it holds.

Together we're a part of this,
A note in nature's grand array,
In every moment, purest bliss,
We find creation's way.

Carving the Cosmos

With chisel sharp and steady hand,
The cosmos takes its form,
Galaxies, like grains of sand,
In patterns dense or warm.

Stars are etched with artists' care,
Planets shaped from cosmic clay,
Each orbit traced, precise and rare,
In a grand celestial ballet.

Nebulae, like clouds, are drawn,
In hues that paint the night,
With vibrant swirls before the dawn,
A cosmic artwork's light.

Across the sky, the comets streak,
Like brushes in the dark,
Their tails, the strokes we seek,
As they leave their glowing mark.

In this vast, eternal sphere,
Creation never ends,
The universe, both far and near,
With time and space extends.

Wonders on Papyrus

On sheets of ancient reed and scroll,
Tales of old begin to speak,
Of pharaoh's might and warrior's goal,
In symbols rich and sleek.

Hieroglyphs of distant past,
Carved with care by scribes of lore,
Reveal the secrets deep and vast,
On Egypt's timeless shore.

Wonders etched in golden hue,
Stories bound in time's embrace,
Of gods and kings, both false and true,
In hierarchies they place.

The Nile flows through inked lines,
Bringing life to each decree,
As deserts yield their buried signs,
For all of us to see.

Through papyrus, history breathes,
In whispers from the yesteryears,
A tapestry that never seethes,
But gently shares, and never veers.

The Oracle's Brush

The oracle's brush sweeps through the air,
With strokes of fate unknown,
Each line a whisper, deep and rare,
From future seeds unsewn.

Canvas bare as morning mist,
Awaits the cosmic hand,
In swirls of color to be kissed,
As prophecies expand.

Visions blend in hues and shade,
Truths obscured yet clear,
On painted lines where fate is laid,
Destinies appear.

Through mystic signs the tales unfold,
Foretelling times ahead,
In strokes both vibrant and bold,
The spirits' words are said.

With every sweep a story lies,
Beyond the mortal eye's reach,
The oracle's brush paints the skies,
Their secrets, softly teach.

Shape of Imagination

In whispers, dreams begin their flight,
In colors that defy the night.
They curl and twist, pure neon streams,
Upon our souls, they cast their beams.

Mountains glow with vibrant hues,
Rivers dance in golden shoes.
Forests hum with whispered songs,
Stars erupt, bold and strong.

Each thought sparks a grand design,
A cosmic blend of space and time.
In the forge of boundless lore,
Shapes of wonder line the floor.

Ideas paint the midnight skies,
Brushes dipped in varied dyes.
Endless realms of vast creation,
Born from wild imagination.

Through this portal, step we dare,
Into visions strange and rare.
In this land, no bounds constrain,
Infinite worlds, our minds attain.

The Potter's Vision

Hands that mold with loving care,
Clay and earth, with skill aware.
Shapes emerge from thought divine,
Softened edges, forms refine.

Each touch a whisper, soft and slow,
Crafts a tale that starts to grow.
From stubborn lump to graceful art,
A piece of soul, a beating heart.

Vision guides the fingers' flight,
Turning dusk to morning light.
Spinning wheel and steady gaze,
Echo dreams of ancient days.

Textures form with practiced ease,
Sculpting life from silent tease.
Earthy scents fill humble thrones,
Creation sings through fired tones.

When kiln's embrace releases hold,
A story countless shades unfold.
From potter's hands, a vision spread,
A tale of life, reverently bred.

Waltz of Brilliant Minds

Whispers soft of thoughts so deep,
In corridors where shadows sleep.
Glimmering paths of wild conjecture,
Dancing upon the sharpest vector.

Ideas waltz in rhythmic grace,
Lit by sparks in a boundless space.
Mentors, sages, souls entwined,
In the dance of brilliant minds.

Binary stars of endless wonder,
Bathed in beams and velvet thunder.
Each turn, each twist, a novel glow,
In spirals vast, the thinkers flow.

Symphonies of intellect arise,
In secret realms behind the eyes.
Paradigms shift, new vistas found,
In harmony's most sacred sound.

Together, bound by insight's thread,
These brilliant minds, by muses led.
Compose a waltz, a mental spree,
In the vast expanse of eternity.

Blueprint of Genius

In the quiet room of thought,
Floods of revelation sought.
Lines on paper, visions clear,
Whispers of a future near.

Every stroke a stroke of grand,
Genius crafted by the hand.
Patterns born from cosmic streams,
Architects of boundless dreams.

Plans align in perfect grace,
Pillars rise in sacred space.
With precision, heavens drawn,
Underneath the coming dawn.

Genius etched on silent scrolls,
Blueprints of the deepest goals.
Structures carve the great unknown,
Seeds of wisdom deftly sown.

In each draft, a story weaved,
Wonders yet to be conceived.
From the mind's profound abyss,
Rise blueprints of pure genius.

Pioneering Imagination

Through misty veils, the mind takes flight,
Beyond the stars, into the night.
Dreams uncharted, visions grand,
In this realm, ideas expand.

Paths unwritten, roads untraced,
Wonders met in boundless haste.
Each thought a spark that lights the way,
Guiding through both night and day.

A realm where impossibles dissolve,
And mysteries begin to evolve.
Colors, shapes, and endless skies,
Within the heart of those who rise.

Challenging what 'is' and 'was,'
Inventing futures, just because.
Seeker, dreamer, pioneer,
The world, renewed, is held most dear.

Embrace the vast, the unexplored,
In each new thought, a gleaming sword.
To carve the way, to shape, to mold,
In pioneering dreams, the bold.

Manuscript of Fantasies

Ink spills forth in magic swirls,
Unveiling hidden, secret worlds.
Pages whisper tales untold,
In their depths, adventures bold.

Elves and faeries, dragons flame,
Each a character with a name.
In the lines, the dreams unfold,
Stories worth their weight in gold.

Castles, valleys, oceans wide,
In this tome, imaginations bide.
Bound between these leathered covers,
Every legend, every lover.

Wisdom of the ancients shared,
Fantasy's stream, unbroken, dared.
Traverse realms with every word,
Voices long ago once heard.

In the silence, in the light,
These fantasies take day from night.
Manuscript of boundless lore,
Turn the page, and journey more.

The Creator's Song

From heart and soul, a tune emerges,
On winds of fate, its path converges.
Each note a brush, each chord a paint,
Crafting worlds without restraint.

Rhythm and rhyme in perfect blend,
Stories through melodies send.
From joy to sorrow, life's refrain,
In the creator's song, we gain.

Changing keys, life's seasons shift,
Every heartbreak, every gift.
Music flows through time's embrace,
Marking moments lost in space.

Harmony in chaos found,
Timeless echoes, bound to bound.
Voice of earth, and sky, and sea,
Cradle of eternity.

To those who listen, hearts will find,
The creator's song, pure and kind.
A melody to shape one's days,
Through intricate and endless ways.

Palette of Possibilities

A canvas white, potential pure,
Awaiting hues that shall endure.
From soft pastels to colors bold,
Imagination's stories told.

Brush in hand, the artist sees,
Infinite possibilities.
With every stroke, a truth revealed,
Mysteries of mind unsealed.

Blending shades of sun and night,
Creating worlds of dark and light.
Textures rich, dimensions deep,
Wonders in the colors seep.

Palette vast, the choices wide,
Where dreams and reality collide.
Through the strokes, a vision grows,
In radiant or mellow glows.

Each color speaks, a silent voice,
Guided by the artist's choice.
In every hue and tone, a glimpse,
Of endless potential's briefest glimpse.

Echoes of Ingenious Minds

In halls where dreams converge and blend,
Ideas spark and swiftly transcend,
Whispers of brilliance softly speak,
Genius found in the minds unique.

Shadows dance, a cerebral spree,
Waves of thought across the sea,
Each echo a light finely traced,
In the silence, brilliance embraced.

Pages turn with fingers deft,
Words of wisdom long since left,
A symphony of thoughts in kind,
Echoes of each ingenious mind.

Labors of love, pursuits so grand,
Every note a mindful hand,
Harmony in whispers, sighs,
In genius, each echo flies.

From dusk to dawn, they never cease,
Ripples of logic, bounds release,
In the chambers, ideas unwind,
Echoes of the ingenious mind.

Painting with Passion

Brush strokes dance on canvas wide,
Colors merge, a vibrant tide,
In every hue, a story speaks,
Passion rises, quiet peaks.

Palette rich with shades untamed,
Dreams conveyed, emotion framed,
With each stroke, the heart entwined,
Painting passions, undefined.

Canvas bare to masterpiece,
Each layer brings a tender peace,
In the hues, the soul ignites,
Captured moments, pure delights.

Deep in night, a painter's trance,
Through colors, feelings perfectly enhance,
Merge of vision, heart, and thought,
In each painting, love is caught.

Artistry in liquid grace,
Passion flows in every space,
With fervent heart, the colors blend,
On canvas, passion has no end.

The Artisan's Heartbeat

Hammer falls with rhythmic glee,
Unfolding patterns, wild and free,
In every strike, the heart's command,
Crafted not by mind, but hand.

Wood and stone, metal's gleam,
Woven into every dream,
Rhythmic pulse, the tools aligned,
Heartbeat of the artisan, refined.

Silent workshop, metal song,
Through crafted pieces, beats are strong,
In the quiet, hands create,
Artisan's love, intricately great.

Each creation breathes with life,
Born from joy, not born from strife,
In the forge, or in the wood,
Crafted with a beating good.

Hands and tools in sync, they dance,
With every piece, the heart's romance,
The true artisan's loving feat,
Is found within their pulsing beat.

Sculpting Shimmering Concepts

Marble waits, a silent form,
To become something beyond the norm,
Chisel shapes, a concept gleams,
Within the stone lies sculpted dreams.

Each cut, a clear and thoughtful stream,
Ideas born, in silent scream,
Concepts shimmer, pure and bright,
Sculptor's touch gives them flight.

Fragmented stone beneath the feet,
In each shard, a notion sweet,
With every strike, a vision clears,
Sculpting through both hopes and fears.

Hands of grace define the scheme,
In hard stone, the softest dream,
Movement captured, thoughts impressed,
Sculpting concepts, heart confessed.

Final form, it stands so clear,
A testament, both bold and near,
In the sculpture, concepts beam,
Shimmering bright, as if they dream.

The Sculptor's Muse

In marble veins the chisel sings,
A symphony of silent things,
Each strike reveals a hidden face,
Emerging from its cold, white place.

The dust it rises, a fleeting cloud,
Encasing forms both soft and proud,
A muse once trapped in stone's embrace,
Now free to dance through time and space.

With hands that carve and hearts that see,
The sculptor shapes what dreams might be,
A whisper in the marble's grain,
A soul released from solid chain.

Crafting the Ethereal

We weave the threads of light and shade,
Patterns in the air we've made,
An artist's touch on canvas thin,
A vision caught, where dreams begin.

Each brush stroke tells a story, bright,
Crafting day from endless night,
The ether sings to those who hear,
The whispers of a world not near.

Fingers trace the star-dust trails,
Crafting magic where vision fails,
With spirit pure and canvas wide,
The universe in colors hide.

Patterns of Thought

In labyrinths of mind we stray,
Through winding paths both night and day,
Each thought a thread in grand design,
A tapestry both coarse and fine.

Patterns stitch through woven dreams,
A dance of light on silent streams,
Ideas bloom in hidden folds,
A story vast that thought unfolds.

The thinker's path is never straight,
A maze of wonder, threads of fate,
Through twists and turns we come to see,
The patterns of our mystery.

Illumination's Cradle

In twilight's arms the shadows lay,
A cradle's calm at close of day,
Soft whispers of the night ensue,
As moonlight paints the world anew.

Stars ignite the velvet night,
Candles of the endless light,
Cradled in the darkened hush,
Where dreams awaken with a rush.

Through ink of night the dawn will seep,
Dreamers rise from slumber's keep,
Illumination's gentle call,
Guiding through the nightfall's sprawl.

A Dance of Imagination

In twilight's hush, where dreams take flight,
Ideas dance in soft moonlight,
They waltz on winds, in vibrant hues,
A ballet born of whispered muse.

With every step, new worlds unfold,
In realms of silver, bronze, and gold,
A galaxy of thoughts, untamed,
In rhythm with the stars, unnamed.

Through corridors of time they sweep,
Awakening the hearts that sleep,
In pirouettes of pure delight,
A dance of fire, spirit bright.

The shadows bend, the echoes sing,
Imagination's boundless spring,
On ethereal floors they spin,
Light as dusk and night's thin skin.

When dawn arrives, they gently rest,
In chambers of the quieted breast,
Yet in the minds that welcomed them,
Their dance will never truly end.

The Artisan's Whisper

In the hush of dawn's first light,
An artisan begins their rite,
With gentle strokes, the canvas breathes,
A life from whispered, ancient eaves.

The brush, it dances, twirls in hand,
As colors sing to desert sand,
A landscape born from fleeting sighs,
Crafted under watchful skies.

Chisel meets the stone with grace,
Revealing form from marble's face,
A sculpture, poised, begins to rise,
A soul set free, no more disguised.

Each creation holds a story, dear,
Echoes of a world that's near,
Through hands that mold and eyes that see,
The whispers of eternity.

With final touches, soft as rain,
The masterpiece is then proclaimed,
A testament in hues and lines,
To whisperings that time defines.

Threads of Thought

In quiet nooks, where stillness dwells,
Thoughts weave tales that silence tells,
Threads of gold and gentle gray,
Spun in patterns' intricate play.

Like silk, they drift on airy streams,
Binding hearts and distant dreams,
In webs of wonder, woven fine,
Connecting souls through space and time.

Each thought, a whisper, soft and light,
A dancer in the soft twilight,
They intertwine in lattice fair,
Creating worlds beyond compare.

From mind to mind, the threads extend,
In bridges that few comprehend,
An endless tapestry, so vast,
Of present moments, futures, past.

These thoughts, a river, flowing free,
An endless source of artistry,
In every weave, a story sought,
Within the threads of every thought.

Colors of the Mind

In the realm where thoughts entwine,
Colors bloom beyond design,
Hues of wonder, shades of gleam,
Paint the canvas of each dream.

Crimson thoughts of passion's fire,
Azure depths of heart's desire,
Emerald shades of nature's plea,
Captured in the mind's decree.

Golden sparks of fleeting joy,
Silver streams of time's employ,
A spectrum vast and ever bright,
Guiding through the darkened night.

With every thought, a stroke is made,
A portrait rich, where feelings shade,
A masterpiece within the brain,
A testament to joy and pain.

Thus, the mind in colors vast,
Creates a world that knows no past,
In every hue, a secret finds,
The boundless colors of our minds.

Threads of Genius

In the loom of night, stars align,
Whispers of wisdom, threads so fine,
Ideas weave, pure design,
A tapestry of the mind, divine.

Through challenges, brilliance soars,
Crafting realms behind closed doors,
In the silence, genius roars,
Unlocks unseen paths, explores.

Each moment, a delicate thread,
Spinning thoughts in quiet stead,
From the heart, not the head,
The unseen path forever led.

Wisdom stitched in hands and eyes,
Genius hidden in disguise,
In humble acts, the magic lies,
Transforming truth with silent skies.

As night turns to day, anew,
Genius dawns in every hue,
Threads of vision, bold and true,
In silence, creation grew.

A Symphony of Thoughts

Within the mind, a symphony plays,
Notes unspoken, endless arrays,
Days and nights, this rhythm sways,
Orchestrating dreams, fond relays.

Ideas dance on air so light,
Mid the dawn and deep of night,
Every thought, a shade of bright,
A masterpiece of silent might.

In the quiet, melodies bloom,
Songs that chase away the gloom,
Weaving patterns on the loom,
Of the mind's vast open room.

In harmony, thoughts combine,
Crafting tales both rare and fine,
Each a spark of bright design,
Resonating through the spine.

Symphonies in quiet crescendos rise,
Underneath, a world that flies,
Boundless dreams in muted ties,
In the heart where music lies.

Dreamweaver's Workshop

In corners dark, the dreamer spins,
Crafting worlds where light begins,
Out of shadows, hope within,
Masterpieces forged by kin.

Every thread a story tells,
In whispered tones where longing dwells,
From the silence, magic wells,
In a realm where dream compels.

Hands of night trace unseen art,
Stitching hope in every part,
Quietly they form the heart,
Of visions poised for sacred start.

Through night's veil, creations drip,
Inspiration on every lip,
From the void, dreams gently slip,
In the dreamweaver's subtle grip.

Eternal tapestries unfurl,
In this ethereal, silent whirl,
Dreams converging, truths untwirl,
In the dreamweaver's world, they swirl.

The Artisan's Cauldron

Within the cauldron, thoughts ignite,
Crafted with both day and night,
Brews of wonder taking flight,
In the artisan's silent sight.

Mixing hues of life and lore,
Ancient secrets at the core,
Shadows weave as light does pour,
Transforming dreams from evermore.

In every stir, a tale unfolds,
Miracles the heart beholds,
With each whisper, life remolds,
In the magic that the cauldron holds.

Textures clash and blend as one,
Under moon and timeless sun,
In this space, the work's begun,
Where all forms of stories spun.

An alchemist's touch, pure and refined,
Molding matter from the mind,
Within the cauldron, fate's entwined,
Miracles rarest, one will find.

The Artist's Glimpse

Colors dance on empty canvas,
Dreams are etched in flowing hues.
Brushstrokes tell a silent story,
In shadows and in blues.

A painter's world in vibrant whirl,
Thoughts take forms with gentle grace.
Each flourish holds a secret wish,
A fleeting smile, a stranger's face.

Palettes blend with whispered hopes,
Untamed as the morning breeze.
Captured moments, fleeting visions,
Time suspended, heart at ease.

In the depths of twilight's brush,
Mirrored soul reflections lie.
Every stroke a yearning poem,
A glimpse immortalized, passed by.

In chaos of artistic madness,
Order blooms in creativity's realm.
Within each frame lies boundless worlds,
The artist at the helm.

Kaleidoscopic Visions

Fragmented light through prisms bright,
Splintering into hues untold.
Perfumed whispers of the twilight,
Memories in colors bold.

Glimmering shards of distant dreams,
Cascade with every breath we take.
Moving in a ceaseless pattern,
In the quiet, our hearts awake.

Shifting scenes of abstract wonder,
Mingle in a dance divine.
Every spectrum holds a story,
Every shade a secret sign.

In the whirl of mirrored moments,
Reflections of our souls reside.
A thousand gleams, a million shadows,
Truth in myriad forms implied.

Kaleidoscopic visions dance,
In the twilight of our mind.
Mojave dreams and starlit whispers,
A tapestry of time aligned.

Threading Thought's Tapestry

Threads of silver, threads of gold,
Woven tales of young and old.
Each fiber tells a whispered secret,
Every stitch is bravery bold.

In the loom of mindful wonders,
Colors blend in silent song.
Patterns formed in gentle moments,
Tapestry of thoughts lifelong.

Interwoven hopes and fears,
Dappled with the light of dawn.
Vibrant strands of past and present,
To the future ever drawn.

Hands of fate in artistry,
Crafting futures from the past.
Threads of thought in endless dance,
Each loop and knot forever cast.

In the fabric of existence,
Boundless tales are richly spun.
In every thread, a universe,
In every weft, the world as one.

Whispers of the Muse

In twilight's hush, the muse does weave,
Soft whispers on the evening air.
Gently calling, softly urging,
Stories wrapped in tender care.

Melodies of olden times,
Harmonize with future's beats.
Inspiration shyly flickers,
At the heart where passion greets.

Words like petals drifting down,
Forming verses, rhythms pure.
Creativity in flowing streams,
Waves of dreams, so bright, so sure.

A muse's touch, so light, unseen,
Guiding thoughts to realms unknown.
In silent moments, sparks ignite,
Seeds of wonder brightly sown.

Eternal whispers of the muse,
Endless fountains, artistry.
In her embrace, we find our voice,
Songs of soul, in harmony.

Patterns of Perception

In the silent pause of night,
Dreams unfurl like silken threads.
Ideas bloom in soft moonlight,
Whispered thoughts within our heads.

Fractals of our consciousness,
Unravel every hidden sphere.
Intricate designs express,
Worlds unseen yet always near.

Memories in spiral shapes,
Weaving tales of yesteryears.
Echoes formed in vivid drapes,
Crafting joys and crafting tears.

Patterns etched in heart and soul,
Rhythms pulsing with life's beat.
In perception find the whole,
Connections pure, connections deep.

The fabric of our inner view,
Woven tight with strands of light.
Truths emerge in colors true,
Schemes of day and dreams of night.

The Painter's Palette

Brushstrokes speak in silent hues,
Canvas breathes with vibrant life.
Every sweep a promise fused,
Captured moments free from strife.

Dabs of color, bold and bright,
Mingle in a dance profound.
Sunrise kissed with morning's light,
Shadows deep where night is found.

Each tone tells a story clear,
Whispers of a thousand views.
Hope and sorrow, love and fear,
All conveyed in reds and blues.

Nature's bloom, in green unfurls,
Azure skies with golden suns.
Windows to the artist's world,
Magic bright on canvas runs.

In this palette lies the heart,
Joined in daubs both small and grand.
A universe rendered in part,
By the painter's skillful hand.

Stitching Sentiments

Threads entwine in woven dreams,
Fabrics rich in thoughts and care.
Every stitch a tale redeems,
Spun with hope and love's repair.

Needles whisper through the cloth,
Guided by a steady hand.
Mending hearts both bruised and soft,
Fates entwined like grains of sand.

Patterns tell of joy and strife,
Interwoven truths that bind.
Moments marked in vibrant life,
Yarns of time in colors kind.

Seams of laughter, lines of tears,
Tapestries of moments past.
Crafted through the tender years,
Where the memories hold fast.

Hands that weave the stories tight,
Giving shape to thoughts unspoken.
In these stitches, hearts unite,
Bound by threads that can't be broken.

Harmony of Ideas

Thoughts entwine in dance of mind,
Waltzing through the corridors.
All together, truths aligned,
Opening unseen doors.

Melodies of wisdom play,
Notes of insight interweave.
Every concept finds its way,
In the forms that we conceive.

Symphonies of light and shade,
Composed with intention clear.
In each harmony, thoughts evade,
Bounds of doubt and clouds of fear.

Resonance in every thought,
Echoed deep in hearts and dreams.
Unified, the silence caught,
In the flow of endless streams.

Harmony of ideas bright,
Shines within the shared collective.
By this synergy, hearts light,
Unified in one perspective.

Symphony of Visions

In twilight's gentle, golden hues,
Fades a dream the heart once knew.
Whispers of winds, the skies embroider,
Nature sighs, its secret holder.

Shadows dance in moon's embrace,
Stars spark tales of distant grace.
Night's soft symphony, calm and grand,
Sculpting dreams in cosmic sand.

Mountains stand in whispered still,
Echoes faint from crest to hill.
Gliding spirits weave and twine,
Crafting visions, pure, divine.

Oceans hum their ancient lore,
Every wave, a tale, a score.
Depths unknown, their secrets spin,
Symphony where dreams begin.

Sunrise nudges night away,
Awakening light heralds day.
Visions fade, yet seeds remain,
Germinating, hearts sustain.

Beams of Insight

Morning light whispers through trees,
Casting dreams on rolling seas.
Insights burst, a radiant flare,
Filling realms with wisdom rare.

Gentle beams caress the face,
Unlocking thoughts in silent grace.
Truths unveiled in fleeting glance,
Guided by fate's gentle dance.

Patterns woven in the sky,
Knowledge gleaned from bird's high cry.
Sun's embrace, a scholar's muse,
In every ray, ideas transfuse.

Stars appear as daylight wanes,
Shining truths in twinkling veins.
Bright reflections of the mind,
In the night, pure thoughts we find.

Celestial whispers, cosmic light,
Illuminate our inner sight.
Guided by the heavens' gleam,
Thoughts converge in mystic dream.

Carved Thoughts

Upon the stone, the chisel's kiss,
Marks of time, in silent bliss.
Every groove, a thought refined,
Shape of dreams, deeply enshrined.

Marble whispers tales untold,
Life's grand stories, carved and bold.
Light and shadow, deftly play,
Crafting wonder, night and day.

Tools in hand, visions emerge,
Heart and hammer thoughts converge.
In each strike, intent does bind,
Artistry, pure and unconfined.

Fossilized in timeless grain,
Moments captured, joy and pain.
Carved in time, thoughts remain,
Echoes in an endless rain.

The chisel rests, the work complete,
Timeless thoughts, in stone repeat.
Silent yet profoundly loud,
Carved thoughts, ever proud.

Epics of the Artisan's Hand

With every stroke, a tale unfolds,
In folds of clay, the story told.
Crafted epic, human touch,
Time and skill, art's gentle clutch.

Wood and metal, cloth and clay,
In deft hands, they find their way.
Canvas vibrant, colors sing,
Epics forged in each small thing.

From raw earth, the visions rise,
Under moon and sunlit skies.
Epics grand with humble start,
Forged in fires of the heart.

Craft and skill in concert blend,
To creation, minds attend.
Every piece, uniquely grand,
Epics shaped by artisan's hand.

Completed work, serene and true,
Old legends with a touch anew.
By the hand of one inspired,
Epics live as hearts are fired.

Chiseling Whimsy

A sculptor's dream in daylight fares,
With chisel poised, a craft he dares.
In every strike, a tale unfolds,
Of whimsy wrought, of forms he molds.

The marble yields to skilled caress,
Imagination's fond finesse.
Through dust and chips, a dance ensues,
Where art and fantasy fuse.

From blocks of stone, life emerges,
As heart and hand, with passion, surges.
Each curve and edge, a story's line,
A testament to dreams divine.

In silent halls, where echoes dwell,
A sculptor's whimsy casts its spell.
With every chisel's touch, we see,
The soul of stone set free.

Within the gallery of dreams,
A silent symphony redeems.
The sculptor's whimsy, timeless, stays,
In marble, caught ablaze.

Song of the Brush

Upon the canvas, whispers blend,
A painter's brush strokes without end.
In hues of gold and azure skies,
A world of dreams before us lies.

The brush in hand, a wand of grace,
Elicits beauty's tender face.
With every stroke, a vision's birth,
Of landscapes rich and hearts of worth.

In shadows deep and highlights bright,
A soulful dance of dark and light.
Each color sings in harmony,
A visual rhapsody set free.

By day or night, in silence spun,
The painter's whisperings are done.
With every sweep, a story told,
In pigment's grasp, wonders unfold.

In corners quiet, light's embrace,
The brush's song leaves its trace.
An artist's heart, in strokes conveyed,
Where dreams and world in color are laid.

The Architect's Vision

In blueprints blue, where dreams reside,
An architect's grand visions bide.
With lines and curves, a future drawn,
From dawn to dusk, their art is born.

In structures tall, their vision stands,
A testament to crafted plans.
Each beam and stone, a thought's design,
In grandeur's shadow, dreams align.

Foundations deep, ambitions rise,
Inspired by clouds that kiss the skies.
From form to function, space unfolds,
A world anew in plans they hold.

In bricks and glass, their stories weave,
A tapestry of what they believe.
The skyline bears their silent mark,
In every edifice, a spark.

With pencil's stroke and careful hand,
The future shapes on their command.
An architect's vision, bold and bright,
Transforms the day and dreams the night.

Melody in Marble

In silent stones, where echoes rest,
A melody awaits, expressed.
With sculptor's hands, it finds its voice,
A testament to human choice.

From rugged rock to polished sheen,
A symphony of forms unseen.
In each contour, a note resounds,
Of creativity unbound.

The chiseling strikes, a rhythm true,
A cadence in each surging view.
With every touch, a chord is played,
In marble's heart, a tune is laid.

Ephemeral and eternal blend,
In harmony, both start and end.
A sculptor's song, in stone made clear,
Each verse a marvel we revere.

So as we gaze upon the shape,
In marble's depth, our thoughts escape.
A melody in stone's embrace,
Eternal, fragile, full of grace.

Sculpting the Intangible

In shadows cast by moonlit tone,
Dreams take shape in hearts unknown,
With hands of thought, we carve and hone,
Imagining what can't be shown.

Whispers of the silent breeze,
Shape the form no eye can seize,
Each chisel touch, a soul to tease,
Creating art with gentle ease.

Beyond the fog where feelings bloom,
Ideas are freed from silent tomb,
Sculpting realms in phantom room,
A dance of thought, a whispered plume.

Music from the stars above,
Guides each hand in tender love,
Sculpting thoughts that gently shove,
Bringing shape to stories of.

As sunlight fades and days do meld,
The intangible, in hands we've held,
Forms unseen by words compelled,
Endless realms our hearts have spelled.

Elixirs of Inspiration

Potions brewed in twilight glow,
Crafted from life's ebb and flow,
Essence of the stars below,
Inspiration's gentle tow.

Dropped in hearts with lightest touch,
Every sip reveals so much,
In the mind, a spark will clutch,
Fires of dreams they gladly clutch.

In the quiet midnight hour,
Elixirs yield their secret power,
Words and visions start to flower,
Binding moments sweetly sour.

Brews of moonlight, sunlit streams,
Gathered from the realm of dreams,
Blend to form those fleeting beams,
Guiding hearts to higher themes.

Sipped in thought, or felt in mind,
Elixirs of a gentle kind,
Lead us to the truths we find,
Unseen paths that twist and wind.

Hues of Creativity

Brushstrokes dance on canvas bright,
Hues that kiss the silent night,
Colors born from pure delight,
A spectrum where thoughts ignite.

Reds of passion, blues of peace,
Every stroke, a soul's release,
Yellows where our hopes increase,
Hues that never seem to cease.

Mixing shades of joy and sorrow,
Crafting whispers of tomorrow,
Every blend a heart to borrow,
Colors of both bold and narrow.

In the silence, tones converse,
Hues of universe immerse,
Painting dreams in vivid verse,
Creativity's endless purse.

From the palette of the soul,
Life's full spectrum, full and whole,
Each new hue, a story's goal,
Colors that within us stroll.

Echoes from the Loom

Threads entwined in twilight's grasp,
Patterns formed with gentle clasp,
Whispers of the past we rasp,
Echoes loom where dreams do clasp.

Every yarn a story spun,
Weaving tales of what's begun,
Fabrics of the heartstrings won,
In the loom where lives are run.

Ghosts of moments, threads that trail,
Woven tight in every tale,
Echoes loud in whispers frail,
Crafting lives in fine detail.

In the weave, the past remains,
Every echo, love sustains,
Through the threads, our lives explain,
Embroidered feelings, joys, and pains.

From the loom, the echoes rise,
Woven through in shades and ties,
Memories seen in new disguise,
Patterns stitched beneath the skies.

Encounters with Muse

In twilight's hush, she softly sings,
A melody that stirs the night;
With whispers soft and phantom wings,
She grants the heart its boundless flight.

Her gentle touch, a breeze unseen,
Composes dreams that waltz on air;
Through shadows dark and realms serene,
She guides the soul without a care.

Her voice, a symphony of stars,
Illuminates the darkened skies;
In every note, a thousand scars,
Transformed to sparks in lovers' eyes.

With every breath, a tale unfolds,
Of distant lands and timeless shores;
In every verse, the heart beholds,
A universe forever yours.

So, seek her out in moments still,
When daybreak bends to twilight's hues;
For in her song, your spirit will,
Encounter depths and dreams anew.

Murals of Discovery

On walls of time, with shades untold,
We paint our quests in hues so bright;
Through every stroke, a tale of old,
Emerges from the cloak of night.

Each color speaks of journeys vast,
Of winds and waves and whispers faint;
In every hue, a shadow cast,
Of mysteries no words can taint.

Our brushes dance on stone and steel,
With fervor born of dreams and lore;
In every swirl, we seek to feel,
The pulse of truths we can't ignore.

The murals grow with every gaze,
As eyes unveil what hearts conceal;
In every line, a secret maze,
Of worlds we long to touch and heal.

Thus, through the art of hands and heart,
We navigate our endless quest;
In every shade, a map, a chart,
To lands where destinies find rest.

Sparks Under the Surface

Beneath the calm of placid seas,
A world of wonders lies concealed;
In silent depths where shadows tease,
A dance of light is thus revealed.

The surface hints at mysteries,
Where tiny sparks in darkness play;
They weave through liquid symphonies,
In search of dreams that drift away.

Each gleam a whisper, soft and slight,
From realms where silence holds its reign;
In hidden currents, out of sight,
They chase the storm, elude the pain.

In every ripple, secrets glide,
Through caverns deep and valleys wide;
Where sparks ignite, and shadows hide,
The universe in whispers cried.

So, peer beneath the mirrored sheen,
To find the sparks of buried light;
For in the depths of the unseen,
Awaits the dawn of endless night.

Threads of Radiance

Through twilight's veil, the threads unwind,
A weave of light in shadow's loom;
With every glow, the heart may find,
A path that winds through evening's gloom.

Each filament, a beam of grace,
That guides the weary traveler's stride;
In every thread, the night's embrace,
Transforms to dawn at eventide.

The stars above, a tapestry,
Of cosmic tales and ancient lore;
In threads of radiance, we see,
The boundless skies, forevermore.

In woven light, our spirits dance,
Through corridors of space and time;
With every step, a fleeting chance,
To grasp the infinite, the sublime.

So, follow now the threads that gleam,
Through twilight's realm and midnight's hue;
For in their glow, we glimpse the dream,
Of worlds unseen, yet ever true.

Lines of Luminosity

In dawn's gentle embrace, the light spills pure,
Upon the silent earth that dreams anew.
A canvas wide, where shadows cease to allure,
And whispers of gold soak the morning dew.

Rays dance like ribbons through the verdant boughs,
Each leaf a lantern in the waking morn.
The sky spreads vast in hues of gentle vows,
A promise of warmth in the day's firstborn.

Mountains echo the sun's silent ascent,
Their peaks crowned in bands of glowing grace.
Valleys smile in the light's divine intent,
Bathed in the glow of the sun's tender face.

Rivers sparkle, like threads of liquid light,
Winding through the tapestry of the land.
In every drop, the day gleams pure and bright,
Crafting with splendor a world that's so grand.

Beneath this sky, our hearts beat in unison,
In the harmony of light's sweet caress.
Each step we take, a luminous vision,
In the endless embrace of nature's dress.

Moments of Muse

In the stillness of the twilight hour,
Whispers of inspiration softly fall.
Like petals kissed by the morning shower,
Ideas bloom within the evening's call.

The night sky twirls in a dance serene,
With stars composing silent symphonies.
In every note, a story yet unseen,
Unfolds within these celestial seas.

Softly the muse speaks in silence deep,
Painting thoughts on the canvas of mind.
Dreams awaken from their gentle sleep,
Revealing secrets for the world to find.

Through quiet lanes of the shadowed night,
Walk inklings of brilliance yet unheard.
In the heart's chambers, suffused with light,
Awakened by a softly spoken word.

As dawn draws near with its golden hue,
The muse departs with a silent sigh.
Leaving behind moments spent with you,
To bloom like stars in the mind's endless sky.

Crafting Epiphanies

In the forge of thought, sparks gently ignite,
Crafting wonders from the mind's still depths.
Truth and beauty merge in the purest light,
    Breathing life into inspired breaths.

Through the alchemy of silent dreams,
Golden visions from the shadows flow.
In epiphanies, the fervent heart beams,
Revealing truths only the soul may know.

Ideas rise like dawn upon the sea,
Waves of wisdom cresting in brilliance.
Each revelation, an epiphany,
A whisper of the universe's essence.

Thoughts ferment in the cask of reflection,
Unveiling secrets with each turning page.
Crafting wisdom through endless inspection,
In the theater of the mind's vast stage.

And when the mind's journey reaches its end,
Epiphanies stand, pillars of insight.
In their light, dreams and reality blend,
Crafting futures woven from thoughts so bright.

Woven Whispers

Beneath the moon's soft and tender gleam,
Whispers weave through the night's silent air.
Crafting stories from the realm of dream,
In shadows where secrets softly ensnare.

Each whisper sings of a tale untold,
A tapestry spun from threads of night.
In its embrace, mysteries unfold,
Woven with whispers, bathed in moonlight.

The forest hums with secrets old and wise,
Leaves rustling with each whispering word.
In their cadence, the midnight owl flies,
Keeper of every secret silently heard.

Winds carry these whispers far and wide,
Through valleys deep and mountains high.
They dance upon the silvery tide,
Echoes of memories that will not die.

In the heart's quiet chamber, whispers rest,
Their woven words cradle dreams and fears.
Each breath a story, a silent quest,
Crafted by whispers through countless years.

Weaving New Realms

In threads of thought we wander free,
Through tapestries of fantasy,
Our minds, the loom, they skillfully,
Weave realms of rich complexity.

Beyond the veil of daily grind,
We chase the stories left behind,
In whispered dreams, where shadows wind,
We find new worlds to seek and bind.

Each pattern spun, sublime, unique,
Each woven tale, a mystique,
The heart's own rhythm, soft and sleek,
Begins a song that words can't speak.

Colors swirl in light's embrace,
Shapes and forms to gently trace,
We craft new realms where stars enlace,
In silent voids, we find our place.

Weaving endlessly, thoughts set free,
We journey through infinity,
Creating realms that none can see,
Alive in boundless reverie.

Imprint of Imagination

Upon the canvas of the mind,
In strokes of wonder, undefined,
We paint new worlds, both bold and kind,
With colors only dreams can find.

Through shadows dark and glimmers bright,
In dreams we wander every night,
The light of thought a guiding sight,
A journey endless in the night.

With brushes fine, we cast our dreams,
Into the ether of moonbeams,
And in the silence, there it seems,
Our fantasies flow in streams.

Each vision born as twilight fades,
In hues that starlight gently shades,
We sketch new lands, with verdant glades,
Where each imagination wades.

An imprint left on time's vast page,
By dreams that never seek to age,
A world where all minds can engage,
In endless flights—to disengage.

Seeds of Genius

In fertile soil of thought we sow,
The seeds of genius, bright to grow,
From tendrils green, new ideas flow,
A world transformed by what we know.

With careful hands, we plant the dreams,
In rows aligned with light beams,
Nurtured by hope's steady streams,
These visions flourish under sun's gleams.

Beneath the earth, in silence deep,
The seeds awaken from their sleep,
In roots of knowledge, wisdom's keep,
A garden vast, where insights leap.

'Tis in these seeds that futures lie,
In verdant sprouts reaching the sky,
Their blooms the answers we apply,
New realms of thought they amplify.

From humble seeds spring mighty trees,
Whose branches dance on every breeze,
Through seasons' change, they bring us ease,
A forest rich with life's expertise.

Coloring the Unknown

In shadows cast by distant stars,
We dream of lands that lie afar,
Where mysteries rest without a scar,
And visions paint where none yet are.

We take the brush of daring thought,
With colors by our courage brought,
In blank unknowns, we boldly sought,
A world beyond the realm of nought.

Each stroke a question, each hue a quest,
In unknown's silence, we invest,
Our hearts and minds to gently press,
Beyond the bounds of how and yes.

In twilight's edge we still pursue,
The tints unseen, the shapes askew,
Where truth and myth in whirlwinds flew,
We shape the colors, old and new.

With every line, the unknown fades,
To form and substance, light pervades,
Imagination never jades,
We color worlds that thought persuades.

Whispers of a Visionary

In twilight's tender glow,
Ideas begin to form.
Soft whispers weave and flow,
A visionary's norm.

Through dreams they lightly tread,
Pulling threads of light.
In the corners of the head,
They dance just out of sight.

Thoughts like morning dew,
Glimmering on the grass.
In colors ever new,
They patiently amass.

In shadows of the night,
Brilliance makes its stand.
Through the fleeting flight,
Her vision grasps the land.

Yet still she walks alone,
In twilight's tender glow.
Her whispers overthrown,
By the ideas they sow.

Sculpting Realities

With chisel sharp and true,
The artist finds their way.
Through marble, stone, and hue,
They carve the light of day.

Each strike a calculated breath,
Towards the heart's demand.
Unveiling forms through death,
Of the shapeless, hand by hand.

Reflections of a world,
In granite softly curled.
From formless dreams, unfurled,
Into shapes now hurled.

A realm within their grasp,
Is pulled from hidden threads.
Between each conscious clasp,
Reality's quiet spreads.

Yet in the breaking light,
The sculptor steps away.
Admiring dawn's flight,
In sculpted stone and clay.

Embroidery of Ideas

On fabric soft and bright,
Threads begin their dance.
Like stars against the night,
Ideas take their chance.

Each stitch a tender thought,
In patterns taking shape.
An intricate, tight knot,
In texture's grand escape.

Colors blend and sway,
In intricate array.
Concepts find their way,
In the yarn's gentle play.

Through needle's rhythmic hum,
And hands that deftly weave.
Designs both large and sum,
From mind and heart conceive.

Thus tapestry's embrace,
Holds the essence true.
Of thoughts in timeless space,
In every colored hue.

The Cartographer's Fantasy

With parchment pure and clear,
The cartographer begins.
In lands both far and near,
A fantasy begins.

Mountains rise and fall,
In ink both dark and bold.
Across the paper sprawl,
New wonders to unfold.

Rivers wind and weave,
Through forests dense and old.
Imaginations cleave,
To stories yet untold.

Kingdoms vast and fair,
Emerge from pen's light touch.
In world wherein they share,
A magic felt as such.

The map's completed range,
A world in quiet repose.
In cartographer's exchange,
A fantasy now shows.

Whimsy in Wood

In forests deep where shadows play,
The trees do whisper, night and day.
Their leaves tell tales of time and tide,
In every branch, a world inside.

An oak stands tall with ancient grace,
Its roots entangled, found their place.
A squirrel's dance on bark so rough,
In whimsy's wood, we find enough.

When moonlight drapes on timbered hearts,
The forest breathes, the magic starts.
An owl's call echoes in the night,
A symphony of soft delight.

Paths unseen by human eyes,
Reveal their secrets with surprise.
In every grove, a story spun,
Where whimsy rests, and dreams are won.

Ideas in Bloom

In gardens rich where thought seeds burst,
Imagination quells its thirst.
With every bloom, a new idea,
In vibrant hues, thoughts grow so near.

From soil of hope, a dream does rise,
A vision seen through inner eyes.
Petals unfold in dawn's embrace,
A symphony of thought and grace.

When dew adorns the morning's face,
Ideas sprout with elegant pace.
In minds fertile, echoes resound,
Where blooms of wisdom can be found.

The scent of thought pervades the air,
On wings of muse, without a care.
In gardens vast, creations thrive,
Where ideas bloom and come alive.

The Calligrapher's Curl

With deft precision, ink does flow,
In graceful arcs, a tale to show.
The calligrapher bends low,
To trace the words with measured slow.

A story born on parchment fine,
Each letter curves in perfect line.
With every stroke, an artful whirl,
A dance of ink, the calligrapher's curl.

In blackest night or morning's glow,
The quill does move, the heart does know.
On paper's edge, the dreams unfurl,
In softened grace, a writer's pearl.

Through every loop and careful turn,
The soul's own voice begins to yearn.
A symphony of silent twirl,
The beauty in the calligrapher's curl.